# How Emotional Problems Develop

with Guided Discussions

**WDA**
*Disciple Building*

Restoring *your*Heart

*How Emotional Problems Develop with Guided Discussions*
Appointing New Leaders, Phase IV-A & Restoring Your Heart

**Copyright 2001-2020 by Worldwide Discipleship Association, Inc.**
All rights reserved. No part of these documents may be used or reproduced in any form or by any means without prior written permission of Worldwide Discipleship Association. These documents may not be changed in any way or distributed for profit. For copyright information or to give any feedback on these materials, please contact:

Worldwide Discipleship Association
(Attention: Margaret Garner)
P.O. Box 142437
Fayetteville, GA 30214 USA
E-mail: mgarner@disciplebuilding.org
Web Site: www.disciplebuilding.org

Scripture quotations, unless otherwise indicated, are from THE HOLY BIBLE, NEW INTERNATIONAL VERSION®, NIV® Copyright © 1973, 1978, 1984, 2011 by Biblica, Inc.™ Used by permission. All rights reserved worldwide.

NOTE: Worldwide Discipleship Association follows Scripture in joyfully recognizing that God created man and woman in His image as equal recipients of His grace and mercy. In the interest of editorial brevity and simplicity and to address the issue of gender inclusiveness regarding pronouns, we have chosen to use inclusive plural pronouns in this document ("they" rather than "he," "she," "he or she" or other constructions).

*Restoring Your Heart* materials make no promises, guarantees, representations, or warranties, expressed or implied, and assume no duty or liability with regard to the information contained here in or associated in any way therewith. No legal or professional services are being rendered and nothing is intended to provide such services or advice of any kind. Restoring Your Heart materials are not intended to be, and are not a substitute for, direct professional medical or psychological care based on your individual needs and circumstances. Although these materials may contain descriptions of psychological problems, you should consult your mental health provider about any personal questions or concerns you have.

| **Author:** | **Development Team:** | **Publishing Team:** |
|---|---|---|
| Jack Larson | Bob Dukes | Nila Duffitt |
| **Editing Team:** | Margaret Garner | Buddy Eades |
| Nancy Higgins | Jack Larson | Margaret Garner |
| Jennifer McClin | Margo Theivagt | David Parfitt |
|  | Lee Tolar |  |

*How_Emotional_Problems_Develop_with_GD_09.15.2020*
Design by Cristina van de Hoeve
Cover design by Patricia Alba-Hughes

# A Welcome from WDA's President!
Worldwide Discipleship Association, Inc.

Hello Friend!

Let me congratulate you on your decision to learn how to take responsibility for the spiritual well-being of others. By making this decision to continue to walk with the Lord and learn about ministering to others, you are opening yourself up to challenges as well as magnificent benefits. These studies on *How Emotional Problems Develop* will help explain how the past affects the present.

This study is unique in that it serves a vital part of WDA's Phase IV discipleship materials as well as an introduction to WDA's Restoring Your Heart emotional healing materials.

My prayer and confident belief is that "he who began a good work in you will carry it on to completion until the day of Christ Jesus" (Philippians 1:6) so that He is able "to present you before his glorious presence without fault and with great joy." (Jude 1:24)

To Him be glory and praise!

May God richly bless you as you strive to grow in Him.

Bob Dukes
President, Worldwide Discipleship Association, Inc.
Fayetteville, GA 30214

# Introduction To Restoring Your Heart (RYH):

Restoring Your Heart is a ministry designed to help people in churches heal emotionally and relationally. This ministry was created for anyone who has ever experienced pain, rejection or disappointment. This book serves as an introduction to the Restoring Your Heart ministry and serves as a foundation for the healing process.

Restoring Your Heart Ministry uses trained lay leaders to help people through a healing process whereby they will have healthier relationships, including their relationship with God. This healing process is implemented in a safe small group setting using workbooks specifically designed for that purpose. The RYH *Processing Pain* workbook helps people better understand their past and experience a grieving and forgiveness process. The RYH *Understanding Emotions* workbook helps people learn an emotional vocabulary and healthy ways of expressing emotions. The RYH *Conquering Shame* workbook helps people understand the effects of shame in their life and how to overcome this stronghold.

Emotional and relational healing is a lifelong process as well as an integral part of discipleship and was modeled by Jesus as He taught His disciples.

To learn more about RYH, please visit our website at: www.restoringyourheart.com.

# Introduction To Phase IV:
Developing New Leaders

As you begin to use the Phase IV materials, it may be useful to refer to *Disciple Building: A Biblical Framework* or *Maturity Matters* for a summary of this phase. The following is a synopsis:

> When a believer progresses to this phase, he is ready to take responsibility for the spiritual development and well-being of others. During this period, Jesus taught His disciples how to live in His Kingdom. In addition, He appointed The Twelve to be apostles, sending them out on their own to preach the Kingdom of God and to minister to people's needs. Mark 3:14-15 summarizes what Jesus did during this phase: "He appointed twelve [designating them apostles] that they might be with Him and that He might send them out to preach and to have authority to drive out demons."
>
> This phase actually had two parts. The first involved appointing and instructing His new leaders in Kingdom principles (Phase IV-A: Appointing New Leaders). The second involved Christ creating a series of situations that forced His leaders to reevaluate their expectations of what it meant to follow Him (Phase IV-B: Focusing On Eternal Things). Both then and now, this reevaluation crisis is pivotal. It centers on leaders choosing either the eternal benefits of following Christ or leadership roles that grant them temporal power and success. (*Maturity Matters*, pages 67-68)

For the leader who is part of the development of a new (Phase IV) leader, WDA recommends forming a discipleship group made up of people who have already completed Equipping For Ministry. (As in Jesus' ministry, this is an "invitation only" group.) These disciples would have already been able to experience and observe what it means to be "discipled" by a leader, been part of a community of Christians, and have seen and participated in ministry activities. As a result of doing ministry, these disciples will begin to identify people they wish to disciple. The discipleship leader can at this point form them into a group where they will learn and be trained while they begin to take responsibility for the spiritual development and well-being of others.

Developing a new leader generally will take 6-9 months, perhaps longer depending on the time and circumstances. The first series of training will include *Living For Christ* (which includes *The Sermon On The Mount* and *Growing In Faith*), *Disciple Building: A Biblical Framework with Guided Discussions*, *A Small Groups Manual with Guided Discussions*, *Disciple Building: Life Coaching with Guided Discussions*, *Team Building* (which includes *Spiritual Gifts*), *Spiritual Warfare-II*, *How Emotional Problems Develop with Guided Discussions*, and *Kingdom Growth* which includes *Parables* and *Practical Outreach* (Evangelism-II). There are also Bible Readings for the disciple to use in personal devotions. WDA suggests completing the books in the order listed above. However, you may choose what works best for you in your ministry.

The second part of this training (Focusing On Eternal Things) features topics related to living in the tension of the eternal versus the temporal, developing a lesson plan, teaching a topical Bible study, leading a Phase III ministry group, understanding the role of suffering, strengthening ministry principles, recognizing emotional issues, living by faith and grasping tensions within Christianity.

# How Emotional Problems Develop with Guided Discussions
Table Of Contents

| | | |
|---|---|---|
| Leader's Instructions For Using Guided Discussions | | a |
| Chapter 1 | Created In God's Image | 1 |
| Chapter 2 | How Problems Begin | 5 |
| Chapter 3 | Sources Of Pain For Children | 7 |
| Chapter 4 | Typical Adult Problems That Result From Unprocessed Pain | 17 |
| Chapter 5 | The Restorative (Healing) Process | 21 |
| Chapter 6 | Four Developmental Tasks | 27 |
| Chapter 7 | Conclusion | 33 |
| Chapter 8 | A Biblical View Of Restoration: Isaiah 61:1-4 | 37 |
| Addendum A: | Development Of Emotionally-Based Problems (Three Column Chart) | 45 |
| Addendum B: | The Restorative Process | 46 |
| Guided Discussions And Case Studies | | 49 |
| Next Steps | | 73 |
| Answers To The Guided Discussions | | 75 |
| About WDA | | 81 |

# Leader's Instructions
## For Using Guided Discussions

The four Guided Discussions for *How Emotional Problems Develop* explain how a person's past affects the present and how problems can result from not dealing with the past. Disciples should **read the assigned portions of** *How Emotional Problems Develop* <u>before</u> **taking part in the Guided Discussion.** *How Emotional Problems Develop* repaces the Pocket Principle™ in this series.

These Guided Discussions can be used to prepare for participation in a Restoring Your Heart (RYH) group. This resource is also part of WDA's Phase IV training. It is important for new leaders to read the content and participate in a small group to discuss and apply the concepts.

Guided Discussions for small groups play an important role in the growth of a Christian with the **major goal being interaction around Scripture.** The goal of disciple building is not just knowledge, but Christlikeness in character and conduct. Therefore, **application is essential**. (Sections "Looking At Real Life" and "Looking at My Life" are application oriented.) At least one-third of the small group discussion time should be spent discussing application of the truth. It is often tempting to get caught up in the content part of the study, but you, as the leader, are responsible to move the group along to application.

Notes to the leader and the answers to the Guided Discussion questions are in the back of this book. The suggested answers will guide the leader to what the main emphasis of the answer should be based on the topic of the Guided Discussion. There they will also find suggestions, cautions, and additional helpful information. Leaders need to read these notes and the answers before the meeting where the specific lesson will be discussed.

Much of the preparation has been done for you as the leader: topics and Scriptures have been chosen, and questions written. However, it is important that you become comfortable with the material so that you will be able to be flexible and focus on the needs of your group. In *A Small Groups Manual* (WDA), you will find information about the practical aspects of group leadership. Please refer to the section entitled "Practical Dynamics of Small Group Leadership." The book is available from the WDA store at www.disciplebuilding.org/store/leadership-manuals/.

# Chapter 1
# Created In God's Image

God has put in all of us a sense, an inward feeling, that we were created for something better, greater and grander than we now experience. He has "set eternity in the human heart." (Ecclesiastes 3:11) We sense this because it is true. We were created for something better. God created us in His image (Genesis 1:26,27), and created us a little lower than Himself and crowned us with glory and honor (Psalm 8:5).

But we also know that our lives fall short of this glory and honor, and we long for something better. Of course, we will experience the completion of what we were created to be only in eternity. But we can also receive more fulfillment in this life. Jesus calls this fulfilled life the abundant life (John 10:10). To experience this fuller, better life we must become disciples of Christ. We must set our hearts to follow Him fully and to put off the things that trap and entangle us in this world.

This booklet discusses some of the ways we can become entrapped and damaged by sin. It also discusses how to become free to follow Christ more fully and completely. In Chapter 8 entitled "A Biblical View Of Restoration: Isaiah 61:1-4" you will find a discussion about how Jesus' ministry applies to people with emotionally-based problems.

## THE SOURCE OF OUR STRUGGLES

We live in a fallen world that is imperfect and unable to give us all the things that we need to live healthy, productive lives. The Bible says that Satan is the ruler of this world (John 12:31) and that non-Christians are blinded by him (II Corinthians 4:3-4) and under his power (Acts 26:18). He is compared to a thief who "comes only to steal and kill and destroy." (John 10:10) Therefore, we can conclude that the world is a dangerous place to live. Part of the reason the world is so dangerous is that it is composed of fallen people. We are all born into this world in a fallen state (Psalm 51:5). In that fallen state we are separated from God and greatly influenced by an internal nature, which the Bible refers to as the sin nature (Galatians 5:16-17) or the earthly nature (Colossians 3:5). Before a person becomes a Christian, they are said to be in bondage to that nature or a slave to sin (Romans 6:6).

When a person becomes a Christian by turning from their sin and trusting Christ for salvation, God begins to transform them to become like Christ (Romans 8:29). This transformation process, which is called sanctification, is an ongoing, lifelong process that is not completed in this life. God gloriously completes it when we go to be with Him!

This growth process is not completed in this life because we continue to have a sin nature as long as we live. Although we can make progress against sin during our life, we will not be able to fully overcome it. We are no longer enslaved to sin. We have a choice, but the influence of sin is still very strong. Thus, we see that the source of our struggles is our own fallenness and the fallen world we live in that is enslaved to sin and Satan.

## CORRECTING AN IMBALANCE

Although Christians universally agree that our three enemies are the world, the flesh and the devil and that these three interact (Ephesians 2:1-2), sometimes we underestimate the impact of the world on us. In particular, we underestimate the impact of the unhealthy environments that we grew up in and have to continually deal with because of the fallenness of individuals and the world. Christians and non-Christians alike are sometimes hurtful in how they deal with one another. Unwise actions and attitudes are often not deliberate, and indeed, many times we are not even aware that we are making mistakes as we interact with others. However, merely the fact that we are human means that we are fallible and will make mistakes.

Often we in the church have failed to understand the full extent of the damage present in people's lives resulting from their past and current living environments. For this reason, we have often not done enough to help people deal with the emotional damage they have suffered. This neglect is not deliberate, but grows out of a lack of understanding about how emotional damage occurs in a person's life, how it affects a person, and how healing takes place.

Many pastors do not know what to do to help the hurting, wounded people in their congregations. They continue to hope that the traditional teachings of the church will eventually bring about healing, but they often don't. These hurting people do not seem to get better, and in fact, some of them actually get worse. Many may eventually give up and drop out of the church altogether.

It has been estimated that 20 percent of the people in the church are struggling with such severe problems that they never make much spiritual progress. Their problems are often obvious to everyone. The bulk of church members, about 60 percent, are able to grow spiritually but are hindered in significant ways because of unaddressed emotional issues.[1] An example might be a person who suffers from low self-esteem and the fear of people to such a degree that they are never able to share their faith with another person. People in this group often do not understand why they are struggling. The remaining 20 percent grow in spite of their problems. However, they do have some emotional issues that affect them, and they would benefit from dealing with those issues.

It is not just church members that struggle with unaddressed emotional issues. Christian leaders also are affected. A church leader who was responsible for overseeing hundreds of churches in his denomination indicated that many of the pastors he works with need to work through similar emotional issues in their own lives.

We in the church need a more comprehensive understanding of how people develop emotional problems and need to provide instruction, support, and opportunities for healing. This lack of understanding is often the result of an inadequate view of sanctification. We assume that when a person accepts Christ the impact of their past has been wiped out. The Bible says, "If anyone is in Christ, the new creation has come: The old has gone, the new is here!" (II Corinthians 5:17) This verse has been used against those who stress the need to deal with the past. Certainly becoming a Christian and gaining the resources that Christ provides gives us the potential and power for change. But to say that our past has been wiped out and no longer affects us is incorrect. We are a product of our past. This is exactly what sanctification begins to heal, restore and change. The transformation that Christ works in us is a transformation from what the past has worked into us. So, in essence, being transformed by Christ is dealing with our past.

When Romans 8:13 tells us, "By the Spirit...put to death the misdeeds of the body," it is telling us to put to death the things we did and learned in the past. So we must learn how to deal with the past in an effective way. It is not enough just to try to stop sinning. We must come to understand what is driving particular sins in our lives. A real key to this is to understand how the past has affected us and how it is presently affecting us. Sanctification involves two parts. One part is to build a relationship with Christ and learn how to minister with Him. But a second, and often missing, part is to deal with the damage of our past, which has occurred because of our own sinful choices and the sinful choices of others.

End Note:

# Chapter 2
# How Problems Begin

Emotional problems usually begin in childhood, and they primarily begin with unprocessed pain. Painful things (events, situations, circumstances, words, etc.) can be disruptive to our lives. And if the pain is not processed, it will cause further problems. According to Scripture, pain that comes into our life through suffering and tribulations is supposed to bring good into our life, and indeed it does, if we are able to process the pain and let it be our teacher. When we deal with painful things in healthy ways, it eventually brings positive results to our lives, such as wisdom and maturity, even though it may take time. For example, if a teenager experiences serious emotional trauma, it may take a long time for them to heal from the damage. With the right help from other people, they can heal and grow from it. However, if they do not deal with it (by denying the pain, minimizing it, etc.) the trauma will probably generate serious problems that will affect them until they learn how to process the pain.

Pain can be our enemy, but it can also be our ally. Without pain, we would injure ourselves seriously. Dr. Paul Brand, in his book *The Gift Nobody Wants* (the gift being our ability to feel pain), gives tragic illustrations of lepers who are unable to feel physical pain. When they injure their bodies, they are not immediately aware of their injury because they don't feel any pain. As a result, they unknowingly continue to hurt themselves to the point that they completely destroy parts of their body.

Pain not only warns us to stop dangerous activities, it also teaches us valuable lessons and shows us where our limitations are. In Romans 5:3, Paul says, "We also glory in our sufferings," and then goes on to describe the fruit of suffering. If we replace the word "pain" for "sufferings," the verse would read like this, "We also glory in our 'pain' because we know that 'pain' produces perseverance; perseverance, character; and character, hope." This verse indicates that if we do not suppress our pain but feel it and learn from it, it will produce positive benefits in our lives. Pain, when processed healthily, can have a positive impact on our lives.

Problems occur when we are unable to process pain in a safe environment. Addendum A entitled *Development Of Emotionally-Based Problems (Three Column Chart)* explains how unprocessed pain creates problems in a child's life that carry over into adult life and may cause life-controlling problems. It is important for hurting people to understand the sources of their pain if they are going to deal effectively with their past. They are also in danger of repeating their experience with their own children. The first column of the chart (far left) deals with some of the ways pain comes into a child's life. (For most people, these issues begin in childhood. However, these problems can result from unprocessed pain that begins in adulthood.) This next chapter, "Sources Of Pain For Children," will explain this left-hand column more thoroughly.

# Chapter 3
# Sources Of Pain For Children

The growing-up process is painful. It is not easy learning to make our way in this world. It is the parents' responsibility to protect their children from grave dangers in life but not from all pain. As painful things happen, it is important for the parents to provide a safe environment for their children to work through their pain and learn from it. Adolescence is often an especially difficult period, but there will be many other times throughout a child's life when they will have to face loss and disappointment. Parents who help their children process pain and grow from it **when it occurs** are giving their children a gift that will serve them well throughout their life.

The following is a list of ways parents may make life more difficult for their children. Parents may not provide a safe environment for their children, or they may ignore their children's needs, or they may add to their pain by not providing a way to work through pain and learn from it. (See Column One of *Development Of Emotionally-Based Problems (Three Column Chart)*, Addendum A.)

1. **Active Abuse**—Active abuse occurs when an adult or peer inflicts harm on a child. This may not be done deliberately or knowingly. The word "abuse" is used to denote the impact on the child not necessarily the intent of the person harming the child. The following are several examples of active abuse:

    a. **Physical Abuse**—This refers to deliberately depriving a child of physical resources necessary to meet their needs or physically harming them through excessive physical punishment. Physical abuse includes actions directed toward the child such as punching, jerking, choking, or kicking. It also includes threats of violence or abandonment as well as witnessing violence done to another. Spanking is not necessarily physical abuse, but it can be if it is too harsh or extensive.

b. **Verbal/Emotional Abuse**—Words can hurt as much or more than physical pain. Often physical damage will heal while the emotional wounds continue to damage the child. What is said and how it is said is very important. Numerous Scripture verses warn us to be very careful with our words (James 3:9,10 and Ephesians 4:29). There is no faster way to exasperate or embitter children than to abuse them verbally (Colossians 3:21 and Ephesians 6:4).

c. **Sexual Abuse**—Statistics tell us that one out of four girls and one out of six boys have been sexually abused by the age of 18.[1] These statistics are just as accurate for those raised in a Christian background. In our experience, when abuse is talked about in a church setting, people acknowledge that they were sexually abused but usually have not begun to deal with it.

Sexual abuse causes more damage than other forms of abuse if left unattended. It is extremely damaging to a child, and if there is sexual abuse in a person's background it may add as much as two years to their restorative process. Sexual abuse includes forced intercourse (vaginal, oral, or anal), sexual touching or fondling, exhibitionism, inappropriate sexual talk, teasing about sexual body parts, showing a child pornography, sexual kissing, knowledge inappropriate to the age, witnessing parents' sexual behavior, and violations of sexual privacy or boundaries of children. Sexual abuse may occur with same sex or opposite sex parents, siblings, relatives, neighbors, teachers, church leaders, or friends.

d. **Emotional Incest (also referred to as parentification)**—Emotional incest, as the name implies, involves a parent-child relationship that is inappropriately close on an emotional level but does not involve a sexual component. One example of this is the parent who feels and acts closer to one of their children than they do to their spouse. They may confide their secrets or emotional needs to the child, expecting the child to give emotional support, instead of telling an adult friend or their mate. Whenever an adult looks to a child for emotional support rather than being emotional support for the child, part of the child's childhood is stolen from them.

e. **Spiritual Abuse**—This happens when a spiritual leader or someone with spiritual authority repeatedly uses their position as a source of power to control or ensure obedience from another person. Spiritually abused people have been taught, either passively or actively, to repeatedly ignore their own thoughts, emotions, beliefs, and even basic physical feelings. They may believe that if they pay attention to those thoughts, feelings, etc., it would be a betrayal of their commitment to God, God's representative, or to a parent. Spiritual abuse can happen at home with a religious parent or in connection with a religious institution when the leader has total authority. It can be unintentional or premeditated; it can be mild or severe.

f. **Negative Messages**—These are messages that children receive about themselves, others, life, and God that are negative and inaccurate. These messages may be unspoken, but the child still perceives them through the attitudes and actions of others. Some examples are, "All men/women are bad," "I'm no good," "People of other races are inferior/superior," "God is a divine policeman waiting for me to get out of line," "You cannot trust anyone," etc.

There are three messages typically present in a dysfunctional home:

- "Don't feel." (E.g. "I'll give you something to cry about," or "Just get over it.")

- "Don't think." (E.g. "Just do what I say.")

- "Don't talk." (E.g. "Children are to be seen and not heard," or "Don't sass me/talk back.")

These three messages tell children that they are "non-people" instead of communicating that they are people who need to be treated with respect.

    g. **Suppression of Independence**—Suppression of independence is a common problem among Christians. Well-meaning parents may over-control, over-correct or over-protect their children. The long-term goal of parenting should be to empower children to be able to think critically, take responsibility, and live independently. Being too controlling or too rigid or doing too much for children will cause them to have difficulty developing normally. They will either have trouble establishing their independence or seek independence inappropriately.

2. **Passive Abuse/Neglect**—By passive abuse we are referring to the ways parents may fail to meet the needs of their children. God created us with needs: physical, emotional, mental, and spiritual. Thankfully, He has provided ways for us to get those needs met. A primary way of getting needs met is through healthy relationships with other people. For a child, parents are the most significant agents in meeting needs, and when parents neglect to meet their child's needs, the result is pain. The child who is neglected or abandoned, either physically or emotionally, does not receive what they need to live a healthy life.

For example, if a child does not get enough positive attention, they may develop poor self-esteem or act out in negative ways to get attention. The effects of this lack of attention in their life may carry over into adult life. They may not know how to give positive attention to their own children thus passing on the neglect to the next generation. Unfortunately, in our society this type of passive abuse is quite common. If both parents work or if they are distracted by other things, sometimes children are left to raise themselves.

It would be easy for parents reading this section to feel that they have ruined their children because of parenting failures.

## 3 - Sources Of Pain For Children

Every parent has made mistakes, but the truth is that most parents have done far more good than harm to their children. God is a gracious God. He overcomes parents' failures by providing avenues of healing for children. He also overcomes parental failure by continuing to change the parents themselves. As parents deal with their own emotional issues, they can lead the way for their children to deal with their issues as they see parents change and become more whole and healthy.

3. **Poor Choices and Sinful Responses of the Child**—Pain does not come into a child's life only through outside sources. It also enters because of a child's poor choices. Because they are children, they have an immature perception of the world, and, therefore, may make unwise, hurtful choices that sometimes lead to sinful actions.

   All children make poor choices at times. However, a strong-willed child tends to push every limit and question everything. This child will undoubtedly get hurt. The goal of parenting is not to over-control this child or to try to protect them from the consequences of their choices. It is to help them go through the hurts, face the consequences and learn from them.

4. **Personality of the Child**—The personality of the child also influences how much they are damaged by the struggles of growing up. All personalities have strengths and weaknesses and can get hurt. However, some children are more sensitive than others, and they will get hurt more easily and more often. Those who fight and will not give in will also get hurt.

5. **Role in the Family**—It has long been recognized by psychologists that each person in a family has a certain role, a part to play in the family. Some of the most commonly acknowledged roles are the hero, the scapegoat, the mascot, and the lost child. (See *Love is a Choice* by Hemfelt, Minirth, Meier for a discussion of these roles.)

Some of these roles are more hurtful than others. The "scapegoat" is a child who often gets in trouble because of their rebellious attitude. Even if they do not do anything wrong, they often are blamed for whatever the problem is at the time. This role almost always results in significant emotional injury. Another hurtful role is the "lost child." This child is very shy and quiet and avoids trouble. They get hurt because they tend to fade into the background and get ignored and neglected. This child may be too isolated and become depressed.

The biggest factor leading to the continuation and deepening of emotional problems is the child's perception that there is no way to deal with their pain. The only way to heal from the painful things that happen is to work through the pain in a safe environment and learn the lessons it can teach. When a child is unable to do this, it sets off a negative chain reaction rather than a healing process. Parents are the primary source God has provided to help children work through the painful and difficult parts of life.

## THE RESULTS OF UNPROCESSED PAIN

So we see there are many potential sources of pain in a child's life. If a child is not helped or taught how to work through their pain in a safe environment then, as the pain builds up in their life, they will do unhealthy things to cope with it. In fact, when a child doesn't know how to deal with pain and learn from it, it sets off a predictable negative chain reaction. The child must do something to survive the pain. There are four common reactions in a child's life.

1. **The Child Adapts to Survive**—There are two common adaptations that the child might make in order to deal with pain:

    a. **Addictive Behaviors**—Addictive behaviors are activities people do to either medicate their pain, eliminate it, dull it, or distract from it. A person may use something to feel better temporarily, like drugs, alcohol, sex, food, spending, etc. Or they may use something to dull their pain, like sleep, drugs, or alcohol. Or they may use something to distract themselves from the pain, like work, cleaning, shopping, TV, video games, etc. Addictive behaviors serve as an external focus that helps a person avoid what is going on inside.

Some of our addictive behaviors are not inherently bad (for example, food, exercise or work). They can be normal and beneficial. What makes them bad is how and why they are being used. If they are being used excessively to avoid dealing with problems or to avoid feeling negative emotions, they are unhealthy attempts to cope.

As pain builds up, the child begins to look for ways to medicate it. The forms of addictive behaviors available to children are usually relatively benign (such as video games or cell phones), but as a child gets older the options become more dangerous.

b. **Unhealthy Defense Mechanisms**—The child may develop unhealthy defense mechanisms to keep from getting hurt again. Some typical defense mechanisms are denial, dissociation, over-eagerness to please, hypervigilence (that is, hypersensitivity to people, emotions, etc.), mistrust of others, denial of a need for others, etc. These mechanisms help the child survive but ultimately cut them off from the real help they need. This will lead to more pain.

An example of an unhealthy defense mechanism is the child who decides to never get close to anyone again because every time they do, they get hurt. As they distance themselves from people who hurt them (which is appropriate), they also cut themselves off from the safe people in their life from whom they need attention. This isolation prevents them from getting their real needs met, and therefore, leads to more pain.

2. **The Child Suppresses Negative Emotions**—If a child cannot process their emotions and thereby release them, what happens to those emotions? They get stored (buried) inside them in the form of stress. This internal stress builds up and usually becomes evident in one of three ways: explosion or over-reaction, hypersensitivity, or lack of feeling.

   One indicator that internal stress is building up is that there is an explosion or an over-reaction to the things going on around them. Suppose a child "loses it" when they reach a stress level of ten. If they have an internal stress level of "seven" all the time because of buried (suppressed) pain, it will now only take a "three" event to get a "ten" response. This is an over-reaction to the present situation.

   A second indicator that emotions have been suppressed is hypersensitivity in areas in which the person has been hurt. If a little girl was abandoned by her parents, as an adult she may feel that her husband is not going to return every time he goes to work although he may have never given her any reason to believe that he would not return. This is caused by the hypersensitivity to the unaddressed emotional hurt in her life.

   A third indicator of buried emotions is that the child has few or no feelings, either positive or negative. (When we suppress our negative emotions, we will also suppress our positive emotions.) A child may numb their feelings and choose not to have feelings rather than to face them. For this child, negative feelings seem too overwhelming to deal with. A classic example of numbing feelings is the person who talks about an emotionally-charged subject in a very detached, non-emotional way.

3. **The Child Develops False Beliefs**—There are a number of wrong beliefs that a child may develop when they do not have an adult available to help them work through and interpret things that happen to them. The child develops an experiential

belief system, a belief system based on their experiences. This belief system will tend to override any intellectual system they learn later. They will believe what they feel more than what they or others assert intellectually. Typical types of false beliefs are: "I am all alone," "No one will protect me," "I cannot trust anyone" (including God), "I should have known better," "It was my fault," "I deserved it," "It is just a matter of time before it happens again," "I can't stop this," "There is no way out," "Not even God can help me," "I will never be happy," "I am a burden," "God can never love or accept me," or "I have no value."

4. **The Child Develops a Shame-Based Identity**—If enough negative things happen to a child without any resolution, the child begins to think there is something wrong with them. They conclude that because bad things keep happening to them, they must be bad, broken or defective in some way. They do not just make a mistake. They are a mistake. This can be worsened if a parent, authority or even a peer is continuously overly critical or, in the extreme case, actually tells the child that they are a mistake. Eventually a tape of self-depreciation and defectiveness plays in the child's mind whenever they do anything wrong. These messages play back in their mind: "I can't do anything right," "I'm dumb," "I deserve what is happening," "I deserve to be punished."

In summary, when a child is unable to resolve the painful things that happen in their life and the pain begins to build up, it causes a chain reaction. To deal with the pain the child may turn to addictive behaviors to medicate their pain or to unhealthy defense mechanisms to keep from getting hurt again. They may bury their negative emotions on the inside, develop a false, experientially-based belief system or develop a distorted shame-based self-image.

End Note:

1. http://angelakwilliams.com/

# Chapter 4
# Typical Adult Problems That Result From Unprocessed Pain

The child takes all these unhealthy ways of living into their adult life with them: the wrong and ineffective behaviors, the buried emotions, the false beliefs and the distorted self-image. This causes even more pain. If these issues continue to go unaddressed, the problems will get worse.

Interestingly, these very problems often show the person their need for Christ. Coming to know Christ usually brings many positive changes into the person's life, but the types of problems mentioned here tend to lurk in the background and usually do not get resolved until they are addressed directly. This is why new Christians often seem better immediately after conversion, but problems surface (or may return) as time goes on. It is not that Christ does not make a difference: He does. And ultimately, He is the answer. However, we must apply Biblical principles to these emotional issues in order to resolve problems.

The second column of Addendum A, *Development Of Emotionally-Based Problems (Three Column Chart)*, lists some of the typical problems an adult will face when the emotional issues of the past go unaddressed. This list applies to Christians as well as to non-Christians. The problems listed in the middle column are really symptoms of the underlying issues that are described in the first column. These issues (Column Two) are what bring people into counseling and into Restoring Your Heart (RYH) groups. People need help to understand the root problems (Column One) and to learn the skills necessary to overcome these problems. They also need support from other people through the process.

The following is a short description of each problem listed in Column Two of Addendum A. This is not a complete list of problems that might occur. People may experience one of the symptoms, several of them or all nine.

1. **Relational Problems**—A person's defense mechanisms, addictions, compulsions, and emotional immaturity will interfere with relationships. As a result of unresolved problems, a person may not have the relational skills to interact with others in a healthy way.

2. **Poor Decision-Making**—Because the person does not think correctly about themselves, their emotions, their needs or life issues, they will often make poor decisions that add even more pain to their life. For example, it is not unusual for this person to be out-of-control financially. In spite of being intelligent, they seem to lack the ability to think wisely about finances.

3. **Full-Blown Addictions**—Addictions, which may have existed in seed form in a child's life, now take on a life of their own and get worse. The pain increases so the addictions worsen. People can be poly-addicted—they use several things to deal with pain. Usually they use whatever is most accessible and convenient at the time.

4. **Needs Still Not Met**—Addictive behaviors, wrong beliefs, unhealthy defense mechanisms and the inability to deal with emotions prevent a person from recognizing and getting their needs met. For example, if a person is not able to acknowledge and feel their emotions, they will not be aware of their own needs, because it is our emotions that alert us to our needs. Even if a person is aware of their needs, the other problems listed here may hinder needs being met. It is only through a healthy relationship with God and with others that a person can get personal needs met.

One result, when a person does not get their needs met, may be that they become driven. Everything they do is focused on getting their needs met. People who live this way are often unaware (consciously) of their needs. They don't realize what they are doing. If a person's beliefs are wrong about what will meet their needs (and they usually are), then they are destined to get on an endless treadmill of doing things that do not successfully meet their needs. Most of us know people like this—they are extremely needy and draining to be around. Yet they may totally deny that they have needs. Their attempts to meet their needs may turn into addictions as they become more and more compulsive.

5. **Abusive Relationships**—If there were abusive relationships in a person's past, they may unknowingly seek out similar relationships as an adult because these relationships "feel" normal. Each of us has several relational systems in our life: original family, present family, work family, social family, church family, etc. A person may enter into or cause dysfunctional relational dynamics in each of these relational systems similar to those they had in their original family. These relationships are unhealthy and will only produce more pain and problems. It is not uncommon for a person to go from one abusive relationship to another, repeating the same pattern over and over.

6. **Depression**—If a person lives with internal stress for a long time and also experiences many of these external problems (Column Two), the stress may become too much. It can cause the function of the brain to change, and the result will be a clinical depression. This type of depression usually needs to be treated with anti-depressant medication. Clinical depression has become prevalent in our culture, but, unfortunately, many people who are suffering from it do not even know it.

7. **Numb or Primarily Negative Feelings**—Negative emotions and positive emotions are integrally connected. Therefore, if negative emotions are suppressed, a person may eventually lose the awareness of positive emotions also. The most difficult emotion to suppress is anger. If anger is suppressed, the person will often be left with only the feeling of numbness. When a person reaches this point, they are actually disconnected from reality to some degree.

8. **Poor Relationship with God**—All relationships are affected by the issues mentioned above, including our relationship with God. The problems which began in childhood (Column

One) usually lead to distorted views of God or negative feelings towards Him. For example, the need to be in control may make it hard to give up control to God and trust Him. It may be difficult for a person to believe that God loves them. As a result, a person may stop growing spiritually and may even regress.

9. **Feeling Out of Control**—As problems intensify, a person increasingly feels out-of-control, even though they may be very controlling. The impact of childhood problems and the resulting adult difficulties often do not significantly hinder a person until they get into their thirties or forties (although this can occur earlier or later in life). Their coping mechanisms enable them to get through their teens and twenties, but as the stresses of life increase and build up, a person's life slowly begins to disintegrate. They "fall apart." It is at this time that marriages and families fracture or the person has some form of emotional breakdown.

# Chapter 5
# The Restorative (Healing) Process

Thankfully, healing is possible. Nothing is impossible with God! The following is an overview of the healing, or restorative, process in two parts. First, we will discuss some of the essential elements of the healing process, and second, the order in which restoration normally takes place.

It is important to point out that restoration is not about blaming problems on parents or others. It is about everyone, both children and adults, taking responsibility for their own words and actions. Even when someone does or says something hurtful to us, we are still responsible for anything that we might say or do in response.

## THE ESSENTIAL ASPECTS OF THE RESTORATIVE (HEALING) PROCESS

The third column of Addendum A, *Development Of Emotionally-Based Problems (Three Column Chart)*, describes aspects of the restorative process. The following is a brief description of each aspect:

1. **End Abusive Relationships**—Before restoration can begin, any abusive relationships must be stopped either by intervention or by separation. If a person stays in an abusive relationship, it will take all their energy to survive, and there will be little energy left to work on restoration. The goal is to create a situation where restoration can take place.

   There may be resistance in the Christian community to separation even when serious abuse is taking place, and a person (especially a spouse) may be encouraged to endure abuse or stay in a dangerous situation. Often separation may be necessary to save the relationship or the marriage before the situation becomes intolerable. Separation can put appropriate pressure on those involved to get help. The church discipline passages in the New Testament (I Corinthians 5:1-13; Matthew 18:15-17) teach the use of separation to bring about positive results.

There is a legitimate time and way to persevere and forbear with one another. Scripture urges us to do so, developing patience. Unfortunately, the person who is the victim of abuse is often unable to recognize it. Therefore, they may need the input of others to identify the abuse and decide on a course of action.

2. **Control Addictions**—If a person has severe addictions, they will not be able to work on emotional issues until these addictions are under control. This is especially true with drug and alcohol addictions. Severe addictions consume a person and prevent them from being able to deal with their emotions since addictions medicate emotions. Therefore, addictions must come under control before a person can make any headway in restoration.

   Difficult steps may need to be taken to control the addiction. In-patient care might be necessary or a Twelve Step group that deals specifically with the type of addiction the person has might be needed.

These first two elements (stopping the abuse and controlling addictions) must be completed before the last seven can be addressed adequately. If there are serious problems in these first two areas they will prevent any real progress in restoration. The last seven areas listed below can occur simultaneously during the restoration process, but for purposes of discussion, we have separated them.

3. **Learn to View and Express Emotions Properly**—Since not being able to deal with emotions properly started this negative process, this is one of the primary issues that must be addressed. Many people need to learn how to get in touch with their present emotions before they are able to deal with buried emotions. They also must come to understand

both what their emotions mean and how to deal with them appropriately.

4. **Grieve Pain and Losses**—As a person becomes aware of their buried pain they need to learn how to process it and release it. This is called the grieving process. They need to learn how the grieving process works and go through this process a sufficient number of times to deal with all the buried pain from the past. The goals of the grieving process are forgiveness and the release of feelings. Grieving losses will significantly reduce internal stress and the ill effects of buried emotions.

5. **Understand Needs and How to Get Them Met Appropriately**—People who suppress their emotions usually suppress or deny their needs as well. It is important for a person to become aware of their needs, realize that needs are acceptable and learn appropriate ways to get them met. Most people who have significant emotional issues have little awareness of what their real needs are or how to get them met. Each person must take responsibility for their own needs and getting them met. It is not an issue of selfishness but of stewardship.

6. **Learn to Distinguish Between Healthy and Unhealthy Thinking and Behavior**—We all tend to see our original family as normal since we knew nothing different. This is also true of a person who grew up in a dysfunctional family. Since we are strongly influenced by our family of origin, we tend to repeat the same thinking and behaviors in our current relationships. Therefore, it is important to compare healthy and unhealthy family systems and relational patterns so we can recognize what is unhealthy and can make good choices rather than follow the programming from our past.

7. **Develop a Correct View of Self, the World, and God**—Scripture says that the truth will set us free (John 8:32) and that we are to be transformed through the renewing of the mind (Romans 12:2). Underlying most unhealthy behavior is a distorted belief system, and it is important to correct the

wrong and distorted views. Our belief system may even be unconscious to us, but it is there. Most people live consistently with what they really believe. When a person's behavior is inconsistent with their stated beliefs, there is usually another belief system (probably unconscious) that competes with their stated beliefs. This leads to inconsistent and confusing behavior. A person's underground belief system must be unearthed and replaced by the truth.

To change a person's belief system, several steps are necessary. First, the wrong beliefs must be identified, and then the correct beliefs must be clarified. Internalizing correct beliefs requires that the person intentionally act on the new beliefs over a period of time.

8. **Foster Healthy Relationships and a Healthy Support System**—Everyone needs a safe and caring support system where they can be honest about who they are and be accepted at the same time. Most people who are struggling emotionally are also isolated from others and have few supportive and empathetic voices in their lives. One of the first things a person in the restorative process needs to develop is a personal support system. The church is a place where that kind of support can be offered to people. Only when people can be fully honest and transparent can the wounds begin to heal.

9. **Learn to Grow Spiritually**—A person with many emotional issues usually struggles with their relationship with Christ. Much attention needs to be given to this relationship. The more Christ is involved in the restorative process, the faster it goes. Each person in restoration should be encouraged to have a personal quiet time, participate in a Bible study and be in a discipleship relationship.

## THE ORDER OF THE RESTORATIVE PROCESS

Another way to look at the restorative process is to focus on the order in which it occurs. The diagram in Addendum B entitled *The Restorative Process* shows this order. The healing process on the left side of the diagram usually must be well established before a person is able to focus attention effectively on the right side of the diagram. The left side deals with working through the grieving process by feeling pain and processing it. The right side deals with the rebuilding process in which a person gains the skills they need in order to live a healthy life and impact the world for Christ.

Point A in the diagram describes a person who is having significant difficulties in life. They may be addicted, feel out-of-control, be depressed, or have relational problems or some combination of these symptoms. This person is often in denial about the nature and severity of their problems. Point B describes someone who is determining the direction of their life, has healthy relationships, and is overcoming their problems. This person is growing spiritually and impacting their world for Christ.

No one wants to be at point A. Everyone wants to be at point B. But how does one go from point A to point B? It is commonly thought that there is a slow upward process of putting off the old and putting on the new. But experience has shown that for those who are deeply wounded, a different route must be taken. They must first face their pain and grieve it before they can begin rebuilding their life. In order to get better, wounded people must first allow themselves to feel their pain. They need to come out of denial and identify the real issues in their lives, especially their losses. Addictions and unhealthy survival mechanisms need to be given up. They need to take responsibility for the unhealthy choices they have made and behaviors they have been doing and discover what is driving them. They need to grieve the losses in their life and learn how to handle emotions correctly.

All this will take time because it involves a steep learning curve. There may be a long period of grieving depending on how much pain they have buried. In the process, the person will learn how to grieve pain, deal with negative emotions, utilize healthier coping mechanisms and overcome addictions. Usually, as people deal with these issues, they begin to feel better about their life and have a closer, growing relationship with Christ.

The second part of restoration is the rebuilding part (Point B). Many of the unmet needs in a person's life come about because they do not have the skills to maintain healthy relationships or to impact their world. Our needs will be met primarily through good relationships with God and His people and having the ability to impact our world for good.

There are several developmental tasks a person needs to complete before they have the skills to relate to the world in a healthy way. Ideally, these tasks are completed in childhood. However, if they were not completed as a child, they need to be completed as an adult so that the restorative process will move forward.

# Chapter 6
# Four Developmental Tasks

As psychologists have done research in the area of human growth, they have identified four "developmental tasks" that we all must complete in our journey towards emotional maturity. They are bonding, separating, sorting out good and bad and gaining independence. This chapter is a brief summary of the information in this field of study. The section on "Sorting Out Good and Bad" and some of its unique insights come from the work of Henry Cloud and John Townsend in their book *Changes That Heal*.

1. **Bonding**—Bonding, which begins in infancy (0-9 months), is the process by which children learn to connect with the people who care for them. Through thousands of interactions with parents, the child develops a sense of connection with them. In fact, if all goes well, the child will see themselves as an extension of their parents and not as an independent person at this point. Throughout this period, as parents take care of and play with the child, a number of messages are normally and naturally internalized by the child:

    1) **I am loved.**

    2) **My feelings and needs are OK.**

    3) **I can trust others to meet my needs.**

    Once these messages are internalized, the child can start to move away from their parents (separate) and still believe these messages without needing to have them constantly reinforced. However, if adequate bonding does not take place or if these messages are distorted or replaced later on, the child will probably have problems connecting with others as an adult. The lack of connection is because they cannot accept love, do not trust others, or are unaware of their feelings and needs; thus, they deny their need for others.

To heal from these bonding problems an adult needs to become involved in a safe group of people where they can be honest and be accepted for who they really are. Within that context they should be able to begin connecting with people and eventually with God. It is usually necessary to successfully connect with people before one is able to develop a close relationship with God.

2. **Separating**—Separating is the beginning of the process in which children form their own individual identity. This happens between 9 months and 6 years of age. During this period children begin to pull away from their parents and experiment with individuality. As they become more mobile, they can do more things on their own. Children are normally able to pull away and still feel connected and secure if they have internalized the bonding messages.

   If a person fails to form a separate and strong sense of identity, they may face some of the following problems:

   - A general lack of self-understanding and direction in life (identity confusion)

   - Relational problems such as being too dependent on others, being too isolated from others, feeling overly responsible for others, or becoming a caretaker of others

   - Significant boundary problems:
     - Allows others to take advantage of or overpower them
     - Takes advantage of or overpowers others

   In order to heal from these problems a person needs a safe group of people who will encourage them to become aware of their true feelings, needs, and desires. Within this context, the group needs to encourage members to not take responsibility for another's feelings, needs, and desires and begin to take responsibility for their own feelings, needs, and desires. They need to understand what healthy boundaries look like and begin to experience them. By establishing boundaries they will better define who they are and who they are not.

3. **Sorting Out Good and Bad**—A person who does not complete this task makes too big a division between good and bad. They tend to see things as "all good" or "all bad." Everything looks black or white—there is no gray. The essence of the problem is that they cannot tolerate bad in themselves or in others. The reality is that nothing or no one in the world is all good or all bad. Everything contains a mixture of good and bad.

   If a person makes too big a division between good and bad, they will tend to have one or more of the following problems:

   - **Deny the Good**—This person has the tendency to see themselves as bad and blame themselves for everything bad that happens. They deny their worth or their ability to contribute anything good. This person may exalt others as better than themselves or judge others as bad also.

   - **Deny the Bad**—Since this person cannot tolerate bad in themselves, they may deny the existence of bad in themselves and blame others for anything bad that happens, while justifying themselves. This person has difficulty acknowledging their own faults.

   - **All Good to All Bad**—This person sees people and situations as "all good" at first, but later, after experiencing problems, sees the same people and situations as "all bad." The truth is that people and situations are good and bad at first, and good and bad later. As a result of this distortion, this person may initially see a new relationship, church, or job as perfect, but as intolerable later, as reality sets in. The result is that they keep changing relationships, churches, and jobs searching for the "perfect" situation.

   Healing will take place as this person begins to see themselves as they really are: good and bad. They must also give themselves grace. Problems sorting out good and bad usually result from not getting enough grace growing up. The best place for healing to occur is within a safe group of people where the person can talk about their "bad" self and have other people love them as they are, less than perfect.

For healing, this person also needs to learn how to see other people and situations from a more realistic perspective. They need to develop more tolerance for the bad that is in the world and need to realize that the ideal does not exist in a fallen world. Not only are they good and bad, but also so is everything else. They need to practice seeing both the good and bad in a situation, institution or person.

4. **Gaining Independence**—This last developmental task has to do with adolescence. During adolescence a child moves away from a dependent relationship with their parents and other adults where they have less authority, freedom and choice, and into an "equal" relationship with them. This process happens slowly. In America it is seldom totally completed until the age of 26. It is supposed to be completed when the child leaves home and moves out of a dependent relationship with their parents. Some adults never complete this task and continue to be dependent on their parents and other adults or continue to feel "less than" other adults.

If this task is not completed, several of the following characteristics are usually present:

- An inordinate need for approval

- A fear of disapproval

- A fear of failure

- A need for permission

- Feelings of inferiority

- A loss of power (often given away to others)

- An over-dependence on others

- An idealization of people in authority

In order to complete this task a person may need to do several of the following:

- Begin to see themselves as an adult, equal to others, with all the rights, privileges, and authority of other adults.

- Begin to question and disagree with authority figures in an appropriate way.

- Start making their own decisions without checking with others first.

- Pursue and develop their talents in order to develop areas of expertise.

If we don't get a good start on completing these four developmental tasks in childhood, we will have some fairly predictable problems in adulthood. Fortunately, if they don't get completed, it is still possible for growth to continue into adulthood. In fact, Jesus, in His healing ministry, incorporated the four developmental tasks as He taught and lived with His disciples. In reality, no one will complete all of them perfectly; it is a lifelong process.

# Chapter 7
# Conclusion

## ALL OF US NEED RESTORATION

We all live in a fallen world (Genesis 3) and we all have a problem with sin (Romans 3:23). We all are wounded in some way. We grew up in imperfect homes and have dealt with things in our lives imperfectly. In addition, there is often little permission in the world or in the church to admit that our wounds exist, and little teaching about how to deal with them.

The degree to which we have been wounded can be looked at on a continuum. No one is 100 percent wounded. They would be dead. And no one is zero percent wounded. People who are in the more wounded range are just surviving. People who are in the less wounded range are coping fairly well with life, but have some issues they need to address.

Everyone can benefit from identifying and working on areas of their life that have been negatively impacted by unprocessed pain or unmet needs. "Everyone" includes pastors, church leaders and counselors, as well as the general population. As we become more self aware and thereby healthier emotionally, we will be able to connect better with God and become healthier spiritually. An additional benefit of healing from past issues is that we can better understand others and the ways they struggle.

## FINDING HELP

It's important to have other people who can help us heal emotionally. We need others to help us gain insight into our lives and give us encouragement and support to work through our issues. Some of us may begin working on issues because of a crisis in our life, but then stop when the crisis subsides. We need others to nudge us to keep working and to not settle for less than what is needed. In addition, it is helpful to work on issues with people who are also working on their own issues. It's encouraging and enlightening to know that you are not the only one who is struggling. WDA Restoring Your Heart groups can be very helpful to this process.

There are a number of options available for finding help. The following is a list of options that may be used at different times individually or in combinations:

- **Personal Study**

- **Personal Counseling**

- **Support Groups**—These groups usually focus on a single issue that all group members have in common (e.g. death of a child, divorce, infertility, empty nesters, families with special needs children).

- **Addiction Groups (twelve step groups)**—These groups focus on a specific addiction.

- **WDA Restoring Your Heart Groups**—These groups focus on dealing with past issues and learning how to process emotions.

## REASON FOR HOPE

We know that with the help of Christ and those who know how to deal with emotional issues, we can all overcome many of the struggles in our lives. Jesus came to heal us as well as to help us grow. In fact, it is quite common that as people heal from emotional issues they experience tremendous spiritual growth as many of the barriers in their relationship with God diminish. The critical event is to begin to recognize these issues and start dealing with them.

## 7 - Conclusion

The church can often provide what people need for emotional healing and is growing in its effectiveness to help people heal from their emotional wounds. WDA has developed a Restoring Your Heart (RYH) ministry that offers RYH materials and group leadership training for church leaders. The goal is to equip leaders to establish and facilitate groups focused on emotional healing (www.disciplebuilding.org). It is our hope that this booklet will further your understanding of how emotional problems develop and some of the dynamics necessary for healing.

# Chapter 8
# A Biblical View Of Restoration: Isaiah 61:1-4

> *The Spirit of the Sovereign LORD is on me, because the LORD has annointed me to proclaim good news to the poor. He has sent me to bind up the brokenhearted, to proclaim freedom for the captives and release from darkness for the prisoners, to proclaim the year of the LORD's favor and the day of vengence of our God, to comfort all who mourn, and provide for those who grieve in Zion—to bestow on them a crown of beauty instead of ashes, the oil of joy instead of mourning, and a garment of praise instead of a spirit of despair. They will be called oaks of righteousness, a planting of the LORD for the display of his splendor. They will rebuild the ancient ruins and restore the places long devastated; they will renew the ruined cities that have been devastated for generations.* (Isaiah 61:1-4)

Isaiah 61:1-4 is of primary importance today for two reasons. By quoting this passage in Luke 4 and citing Himself as the One to fulfill the prophecy, Jesus clearly states that He is the promised Messiah and King of the Jews with authority to redeem and deliver. This passage also sets forth six key aspects of Christ's ministry of redemption and proposes (by implication) how they apply to His church. In effect, Jesus was claiming to be the Messiah and describing the nature of His ministry at the same time. We need to take a closer look at this passage in order to see the significance of what He was saying and how it applies to people with emotionally-based problems.

The Messianic passages in the Old Testament fall into two categories: one emphasizes that the Messiah would come as a "conquering king" or "deliverer"; the second describes the Messiah as a divine servant who would suffer and secure redemption for the people of Israel. Ironically, both descriptions refer to Jesus. The role of "suffering servant" describes Jesus in His first coming, while the role of "conquering king" refers to Jesus in His second coming. The Jews, as a whole, did not recognize

Christ's first coming, and subsequently, are still looking for the Messiah to appear.

At the time of Christ, the Israelites were weary of foreign dominion. They had not experienced political freedom for centuries. After the Babylonian captivity they struggled with Greek control followed by Roman occupation. It is little wonder that the idea of a Messiah who would appear as a conquering king resonated with them. Unfortunately this emphasis caused them to minimize the Messiah's other role as suffering servant.

Chapter 61 is one of several passages in Isaiah that describes the Messiah as a "suffering servant." Others include Isaiah 42:1-4, 49:1-6, 50:4-9, 52:13-15, and Chapter 53. The Jews generally applied these passages to themselves as a nation, claiming that they were the "suffering servant." Most scholars agree that these passages refer instead to a man often identified as the "Servant of God." This Servant, the Messiah, was also appointed to be the mediator of a new covenant, the light of the Gentiles, the salvation of God for the whole world, and the one who would reach this glorious height through servanthood, a service leading to death.

## SIX ASPECTS OF CHRIST'S MINISTRY

Isaiah 61:1-4 describes many of the same elements contained in this booklet. Jesus quoted this passage at the beginning of His ministry in Luke 4:17-21 to both explain and underscore the nature of His ministry. He concluded by saying, "Today this Scripture is fulfilled in your hearing," indicating, as we will explain, that His ministry was designed, at least in part, to bring about healing from emotionally-based problems that result from the damages of sin. In these verses, Jesus mentions six components of His ministry that relate to healing emotional issues:

1. Proclaim the good news to the poor
2. Bind up the brokenhearted
3. Proclaim freedom to the captives
4. Proclaim release from darkness for the prisoners
5. Proclaim the year of the Lord's favor/day of vengeance

6. Comfort all who mourn

**The first aspect of Christ's ministry that contributes to restoration from emotional damage is the gospel message**, or good news. Jesus proclaimed God's love and forgiveness wherever He went, seeking to draw people to Himself for salvation. Becoming a Christian is foundational to the restorative process. Non-Christians can heal to some degree, but people cannot heal fully until they experience His forgiveness and the new birth He offers.

A lack of forgiveness is a root cause of ongoing feelings of condemnation and is detrimental to the restorative process. To fully experience healing, we must receive forgiveness from God, forgive ourselves and forgive others. Jesus' death and resurrection provides the only real basis for substantial forgiveness.

It is not coincidental that God's offer of forgiveness was directed (initially) toward the poor. Everyone needs forgiveness, but people who have experienced poverty in any of its forms are usually more aware of their need for help and forgiveness. The ability to acknowledge and receive forgiveness as a free gift from God through Christ is the starting point for further restoration.

**The second aspect of Christ's ministry is "to bind up the brokenhearted."** In this passage, "brokenhearted" refers to people who have been deeply hurt (wounded in the heart) and in need of emotional healing. Taking our hurts directly to Christ promotes healing. He is, after all, a suffering servant who understands our hurts (Hebrews 4:15-16). Christ also means for His church to be a place where healing can occur (I Corinthians 12:26). Wounded people need a safe environment where they feel emotionally protected as they express their hurts and receive validation from caring friends. People need to be able to grieve their losses in the presence of their Lord and also in fellowship with His people.

**The third aspect of Christ's ministry is "to proclaim freedom to the captives."** Through His death and resurrection Christ defeated Satan and set His people free. There are two dimensions that were affected by this liberation. The first deliverance occurred in the spiritual realm and has a spiritual application, the second occurs in everyday life and has a very practical application.

In Scripture the spiritual dimension is also referred to as "the invisible realm." Though we can't see this dimension, it is a very real and substantial place. In this realm, Christ set us free in a very real and dramatic sense. Scripture asserts emphatically that Christians have been delivered from the dominion of Satan and brought into the Kingdom of God (Colossians 1:13). This deliverance means that Satan no longer has the legal, or moral, right to control or condemn the children of God. We may or may not experience this new freedom, but it remains true and substantive nonetheless. The implications are profound. The Kingdom of God is a place of freedom. We are no longer slaves to sin (Romans 6:6; John 8:31-36), no longer captives.

Christ also intends that we experience His freedom in the visible world. It is not enough that we simply understand the truth that the evil one no longer has authority to control and manipulate us, or that indwelling sin no longer dictates our choices. Christ wants us to experience this truth regarding our deliverance in a real and substantial way. There is a practical dimension involved in this deliverance.

Though legally defeated, Satan continues to exert his control over people, holding them captive in two ways. The first way is through the "schemes of the devil," habitual strategies that we have embraced in an attempt to offset the effects of sin. They evolve into addictions and defense mechanisms that people use to address unprocessed pain. If we continue to use old mechanisms to deal with our pain rather than rely upon Christ, we remain (literally) in bondage to them, to sin, and to the evil one. This passage reminds us that Jesus came to set us free from these unhealthy ways of living. Through His guidance and power we can recognize and replace these unhealthy practices with more effective and healthy ways of living.

But there is a second way that the enemy keeps us captive. In addition to encouraging addictions that can persist long after people accept Christ, Satan also blinds people to truth, effectively keeping them prisoners in the dark. But Christ wants to release us from the captivity of darkness. **This fourth aspect of His ministry, "to proclaim release from darkness for the prisoners," is what we will now consider.**

Scripture states that Satan has the power to blind non-Christians (II Corinthians 4:4) and does so very effectively, preventing them from seeing the truth about Christ and His Kingdom. However, at salvation Satan's power to keep people in the dark is removed. In addition to being set free from the dominion of Satan, we are also set free from the darkness of unbelief. Now we have the capacity to see things clearly.

Satan's blinding activities continue to exist and can remain effective even after people accept Christ. These activities occur directly through spiritual attacks, and indirectly through a world system of lies that Satan retains control over until Christ returns. These strategies are intended to confuse and mislead Christians, keeping them away from Christ and, in effect, prisoners of the evil one. Over time they evolve into belief systems, strongly held emotional convictions that shape our view of the world, others, and ourselves. Though Christians now have the capacity to recognize these lies, they often fail to because they have not trained themselves to discern good from evil. Jesus came to lead us out of the darkness into the light. The light is the truth. It is the truth that sets us free. Part of the process of healing from the damages of sin involves increasingly replacing wrong beliefs with the truth.

When first studying these verses in Isaiah, one might see them as a paradigm for promoting healing ministries in the church, with the descriptions representing the needs of different groups of people needing different kinds of help. But upon further research, it becomes clear that everyone (to some degree) has all these needs, and everyone is in need of healing in each area.

Everyone needs Christ for salvation and for forgiveness and deliverance from sin. Everyone needs to process unresolved pain and learn how to deal with emotions correctly. Everyone needs God's direction and power to deal with the addictions and unhealthy defense mechanisms they use to deal with pain. Everyone also needs help replacing wrong beliefs with the truth. Isaiah 61:1-2 describes the restoration Christ brings to all people, and His ministry is designed to provide healing in all areas. Incidentally, these are the same areas keeping people in bondage (see "The Results Of Unprocessed Pain" in Chapter 3 and Addendum A).

Built into Christ's ministry was a restorative process that heals the damage of sin. During His earthly ministry, Christ introduced a restorative process that roughly parallels the early stages of human relational/emotional formation identified by many childhood development specialists. This restorative process, carried out in a small group that imitates many of the dynamics of the family-of-origin, provided a safe environment for dealing with wounds and reinforcing the tasks associated with healthy development.

We must remember that Jesus does not deliver us from all of the damage instantaneously. Though forgiveness is granted at the moment of salvation, it may take time for people to fully realize it or appreciate it. The other areas (unprocessed pain, addictions, defense mechanisms, and false belief systems) may take even longer to correct. In truth, some of these may be so ingrained that we struggle with them for the remainder of our time on earth. However, for sustained spiritual growth to occur, we must continue to heal from the damages of sin in these areas.

**The fifth aspect of Christ's ministry is "to proclaim the year of the Lord's favor and the day of vengeance of our God."** The day will come when Jesus will return to gather His people and reward them for what they suffered on His behalf. Conversely, He will dispense wrath to those who rejected Him. Everyone will receive their just reward, either for good or evil (Romans 2:5-11). Armed with the knowledge that God offers forgiveness but that

He will eventually punish all evil enables those who have been hurt to forgive those who hurt them. They realize it is not their responsibility, or prerogative, to take revenge (Romans 12:19). Only God can right all the wrongs.

**The sixth and last aspect of Christ's ministry is "to comfort all who mourn."** Mourning is not a pleasant experience. Grieving our losses causes us to feel depressed or sad. However, this process is a necessary step in healing us from the damages of sin. Jesus promises to be an ever-present help in trouble (Psalm 46:1) and a comfort for people who mourn (Matthew 5:4). In Isaiah, He also promises "to bestow on them a crown of beauty instead of ashes, the oil of joy instead of mourning, and a garment of praise instead of a spirit of despair." This describes what happens after people complete the grieving process: (viz.) they begin to live again. They are able to feel joy (gladness). Their countenance changes (beauty) because they feel better and have been released from the stress caused by buried emotions. They want to give praise to their God.

## THE IMPACT OF A HEALING (RESTORING YOUR HEART) MINISTRY

The good thing is that more happens than just this. When people have experienced significant healing, they are able to grow into healthy and solid Christians. The prophet Isaiah calls them "oaks of righteousness, a planting of the Lord for the display of his splendor." Without healing, believers will remain forever crippled, less than what God has designed. This is extremely sad, for all Christians can become "oaks of righteousness."

Isaiah goes on to say that those who have been healed in these significant ways, and who have grown up, becoming "oaks of righteousness," will be the ones who will "rebuild the ancient ruins and restore the places long devastated; they will renew the ruined cities that have been devastated for generations." In other words, these people will have the knowledge, wholeness, and ability to affect healing throughout their culture. They will be able to reverse generations of moral decay and devastation. They will be able to reverse the effects of the sins of the fathers, which have been passed along to the third or fourth generation (Exodus 20:5).

They will be able to rebuild the culture in a healthy and godly manner, bringing Christ's healing ministry everywhere they go. They foster revival and renewal for generations to come (Exodus 20:6). This healing process is not an option for Christians. It is the plan Jesus left for us to follow. It is our only hope to restore the church to her healthy role and reverse the degeneration of our culture, or any culture. Jesus is willing to bring about healing for those who enter into the process He has laid out for us. The choice is ours. What will we do?

# Addendum A

## DEVELOPMENT OF EMOTIONALLY-BASED PROBLEMS
(Three Column Chart)

| CHILDHOOD → | ADULTHOOD → | ADULTHOOD |
|---|---|---|
| **SOME CAUSES OF CHILDHOOD PAIN** | **EXAMPLES OF ADDITIONAL PROBLEMS EXPERIENCED IN ADULTHOOD** | **ASPECTS OF THE RESTORATIVE PROCESS** |
| 1. Active abuse<br>2. Neglect (unmet needs)<br>3. Child's poor choices and sinful responses<br>4. Personality of the child<br>5. Role in the family<br><br>↓<br><br>**RESULTS OF NOT BEING ABLE TO PROCESS PAIN**<br><br>1. Adaptation to survive<br>   a. Addictive behaviors<br>   b. Defense mechanisms<br>2. Suppression of negative emotions<br>3. Development of false belief systems<br>4. Development of a shame-based identity | Mounting on top of the unprocessed childhood pain, making the pain worse<br><br>1. Relational problems<br>2. Poor decision-making<br>3. Full-blown addictions<br>4. Needs still not met<br>5. Abusive relationships<br>6. Depression<br>7. Numb or primarily negative feelings<br>8. Poor relationship with God<br>9. Feeling out of control | 1. End abusive relationships<br>2. Control addictions<br>3. Learn to properly view and express emotions<br>4. Grieve pain and losses<br>5. Understand needs and meet them appropriately<br>6. Learn to distinguish between healthy and unhealthy thinking and behavior<br>7. Develop a healthy view of self, the world and God<br>8. Foster healthy relationships and a healthy support system<br>9. Learn to grow spiritually |

# Addendum B

## THE RESTORATIVE PROCESS

*The healing process might initially feel worse before it feels better. This is normal. But keep going! There is freedom and life on the other si*

**START OF RESTORATIVE PROCESS**
(POINT A)

**1. PERSONAL DISCOVERY**
- Coming out of denial
- Identifying problems
- Exerting control over addictions

*GRIEVING*

*REBUILDING*

**2. GRIEVING PAIN**

**ELEVATED LEVEL
OF EMOTIONAL
HEALTH & FREEDOM
(POINT B)**

Creating a healhy support system
Giving self and other more grace
Trying new ways of thinking
Learning relational skills
Working on developmental tasks
Understanding personal identity

REBUILDING

Gaining independence
↑
Sorting out the good and bad
↑
Separating
↑
Bonding

## 3. UNDERSTANDING DEVELOPMENTAL TASKS

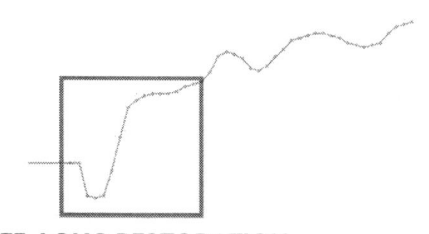

**LIFE-LONG RESTORATION**

# How Emotional Problems Develop
# Guided Discussions And Case Studies
Table Of Contents

| | | |
|---|---|---|
| Session 1 | Understanding Root Causes Of Emotional Problems | 51 |
| | Case Study #1 | 55 |
| Session 2 | Healing From Emotional Issues | 57 |
| | Case Study #2 | 61 |
| Session 3 | The Church's Role In Restoration | 63 |
| Session 4 | Recap Of *How Emotional Problems Develop* | 67 |
| | Case Study #3 | 71 |
| | Next Steps | 73 |
| | Answers To The Guided Discussions | 75 |

# Guided Discussions And Case Studies

The following questions are designed for group discussion and will help you better understand the concepts discussed in this booklet. The group members should answer the questions in advance before they gather for discussion.

The discussions are divided into four sessions. Allow two hours of discussion time for each of the four sessions. There are also Case Studies included to aid in understanding the RYH process. Interacting with these questions and the booklet, *How Emotional Problems Develop*, in a group setting will provide people with a general overview of emotional healing. Understanding this process is foundational to beginning a WDA Restoring Your Heart (RYH) ministry, participating in a RYH workbook experience or developing as a new discipleship leader.

NOTE: *How Emotional Problems Develop* and the following questions and case studies could be discussed in a mixed-gender group. All other Restoring Your Heart group experiences will be gender specific groups.

# Guided Discussion
# Understanding Root Causes Of Emotional Problems—#1

This discussion is based on Chapters 1, 2 and 3 and Addendum A of *How Emotional Problems Develop*. Group members should read the material before participating in this discussion.

## GOAL:

For a person to begin to understand the primary cause of their emotional problems and how they affect their own life.

## GETTING STARTED:

Think of someone you know who has many difficulties managing life. What do you know about their childhood experiences?

How might their childhood experiences have contributed to their present struggles?

**Transition:** Childhood pain that is not dealt with in healthy ways often produces problems in adult life.

Guided Discussion

## THINKING TOGETHER:

1. As you reflect over the first three chapters of *How Emotional Problems Develop*, share any new ideas that caught your attention.

2. Why do you think unprocessed pain causes so much trouble for a child?

3. "Pain can be our enemy, but it can also be our ally." (From Chapter 2.) Explain in your own words what you think this quote means.

   Describe a situation in your own life in which God made pain your ally (i.e. God used pain for a positive purpose).

How can unprocessed pain from the past become an ally? Look at Romans 5:3.

4. What are some of the things a parent can do to help a child develop a healthy approach to dealing with pain?

We must remember that we cannot totally prevent a child from experiencing pain, and, in fact, it would not be good for the child if we did so.

## LOOKING AT REAL LIFE:

5. Explain how you think emotional problems impact our society.

6. How is the Christian church affected by these emotional problems?

Guided Discussion

## LOOKING AT MY LIFE:

What are some ways your life has been affected by your own emotional problems?

List any childhood difficulties that may have contributed to these problems in your life.

# For Further Discussion
# Case Study #1

*Peter grew up in a fairly small town in South Carolina. His parents were well respected in the community. His dad was an insurance salesman and his mother was chairman of the Board of Education. His family rarely ate meals together; even when they did, they were usually engaged on their cell phones. They did not share much with each other about their lives or their feelings but did occasionally discuss politics. Peter's parents pressured him to do well in sports and academics.*

*Peter was the oldest child and was a straight-A student. He wrote articles for the school newspaper about political issues. He was also the quarterback for the school football team. When he finished a game, his dad would tell him he had done a good job but would also discuss with him how he could have done better. Once when Peter brought a girl home to meet his family, his father told the young lady how surprised he was that Peter had become a football player because when he was young he could never catch the ball when his dad threw it to him. This was very embarrassing to Peter.*

*Peter was valedictorian of his high school class. The night he graduated, his parents had a party for him. His father gave a toast saying, "Peter, we are so proud of you, but you could have made your speech without so many 'um's' in it." He laughed as if this was very funny and then added, "To Peter!" Peter did not feel honored only humiliated, but he buried his pain and anger because emotions were seen as a sign of weakness in his family.*

*Peter had always wanted to be a lawyer and soon became one. He moved to a larger town, got married, and started a very successful law firm, but he did not feel fulfilled. He never got over feeling anxious each time he had a court date and secretly felt inferior to other people. He was also struggling in his marriage. His wife, Sarah, would tell him he was too critical of her.*

*By the time he was forty he felt truly depressed and believed that he was basically a failure at everything. He decided to talk to his pastor about his anger problem. His pastor gave him Scriptures to memorize and told him to ask God for forgiveness for this problem. Peter did as he was told but was still acting out his anger in inappropriate ways. He felt ashamed of his emotions and actions and isolated from others. He began staying at work later and later and demanding that his employees work longer too. He felt hopeless and lonely even though people saw him as a confident and successful man.*

## CASE STUDY #1—QUESTIONS FOR DISCUSSION

1) What problems would you say Peter has?

2) What were some of the contributing factors to his problems?

# Guided Discussion
# Healing From Emotional Issues—#2

This discussion is based on Chapters 4, 5 and 6 and Addendums A and B of *How Emotional Problems Develop*. Group members should read the material before participating in this discussion and should also be prepared to explain the chart in Addendum A to a partner.

## GOALS:

For a person to begin to recognize the adult symptoms of emotional problems and begin to understand the emotional healing process.

For a person to be able to explain the chart in Addendum A to another person.

## GETTING STARTED:

Share a situation in which you have dealt with issues from your past in a healthy way and how it helped you (perhaps by forgiving someone, rejecting a false belief, grieving a loss, etc.).

**Transition:** Many people say we should not be focusing on the past. But, if the past is affecting the present, then it does need to be addressed.

Guided Discussion

## THINKING TOGETHER:

1. Based on your reading and your experience, what are some ways the past can affect the present and the future?

2. What are the four developmental tasks? (Chapter 6)

   What are some of the problems that may be seen in adulthood if these tasks are not completed?

   Bonding:

   Separating:

   Sorting Out Good and Bad:

   Gaining Independence:

3. As you look at the restorative process (Chapter 5), explain why each element listed below is important.

   Stop abusive relationships:

   Control addictions:

   Learn to view and express emotions properly:

   Grieve pain and losses:

   Understand needs and how to get them met appropriately:

   Learn to distinguish between healthy and unhealthy thinking and behavior:

   Develop a correct view of self, the world and God:

   Develop healthy relationships and a healthy support system:

   Learn to grow spiritually:

## LOOKING AT REAL LIFE:

4.  The chart in Addendum A, *Development Of Emotionally-Based Problems (Three Column Chart)*, can be used to help people understand why they have emotional problems. For this reason, we want you to be able to explain the chart to someone.

    Find a partner and take turns explaining the chart in Addendum A to each other as if you are explaining it to someone who needs to understand why they are struggling with emotional issues.

## LOOKING AT MY LIFE:

Ask God to bring to mind people in your life who manifest symptoms of emotional problems (See Column Two of Addendum A and Developmental Tasks in Chapter 6). Write down their names and a few of their symptoms. Do not share this list with anyone.

Pray for each of these individuals during this coming week. The next lesson will focus on resources that can be used to help people with emotional problems.

# For Further Discussion
# Case Study #2

*When he was in school Peter was always very popular with both men and women. Before he was married he had dated a lot and there were always guys who were his buddies. He felt especially close to his fellow football players but later had to admit that football was all they had in common. As he graduated from one school and moved on to the next he never kept up with the friends he had met from each school. Now that he has his own law firm and is the boss, he feels it is best not to be too close to any of his employees. His wife has mentioned more than once that she wishes they were closer, but Peter does not understand this. After all, they are married, live together and have two children. Doesn't that mean that they are close?*

*At the law firm, everyone knows there is nothing to be gained by disagreeing with Peter. He will systematically and logically explain to you in detail why he is right. There was one associate who was not intimidated by Peter. He would disagree with him from time to time. After a few months of this, Peter told him that he thought it would be best if he left the firm, and he did. Peter has remarked occasionally, "I thought that guy was going to be great but he turned out to be bad news."*

*The funny thing is that despite his outward confident manor, Peter is very insecure on the inside. He actually feels that many people in the firm are smarter or more capable than he is. One of the reasons he is so driven is that he has a secret fear that the firm will "go under" one day. He doesn't think he could face his father if his firm were to fail.*

## CASE STUDY #2—QUESTIONS FOR DISCUSSION

1) What developmental tasks are incomplete in Peter's life?

   Bonding:

   Separating:

   Sorting Out Good and Bad:

   Gaining Independence and Maturity:

2) Why do you feel that the ones you chose are incomplete in Peter's life?

# Guided Discussion
# The Church's Role In Restoration—#3

This discussion is based on Chapter 7 and 8 of *How Emotional Problems Develop*. Group members should read the material before participating in this discussion.

## GOALS:

For a person to understand the implications of Isaiah 61:1-4.
For a person to know where to find restorative help for themself and for others.

## GETTING STARTED:

In your experience, how do churches approach emotional problems?

**Transition:** God wants the church to be a part of the healing process as seen in Isaiah 61:1-4.

## THINKING TOGETHER:

**Read Isaiah 61:1-4.**

1. Jesus read from this passage to describe His future ministry. Based on these verses, what were Jesus' goals in ministry?

Guided Discussion

2. According to these verses, what should be the result of a restorative ministry?

3. If Jesus said that healing is to be an important part of His ministry, what does that say to the church today?

## LOOKING AT REAL LIFE:

4. What might a healing ministry look like in a church?

5. Does the church need to offer a ministry to accomplish every aspect of healing and restoration? Explain your answer.

6. Brainstorm about what resources are available in your church and community to help a person heal from emotional problems? Begin to compile a list of resources for future use. (Use the list in Chapter 7 for reference.)

7. What are some ways we can all be a part of the healing process in the body of Christ?

## LOOKING AT MY LIFE:

Refer back to the list of people you were praying for this past week. What role might you play in the healing process for each of these people?

# Guided Discussion
# Recap Of
# *How Emotional Problems Develop*—#4

This discussion is based on *How Emotional Problems Develop* with special emphasis on Chapter 5 and Addendum B, *The Restorative Process*. Group members should read the material before participating in this discussion.

## GOAL:

For a person to gain a more complete understanding of the restorative process and begin to identify where they are in the process in their own life.

## GETTING STARTED:

Reflect on your experience beginning a new job. What was the process you went through in order to become competent in the job?

**Transition:** In the same way, healing from our past wounds is a process that has many aspects to it.

## THINKING TOGETHER:

1. Look at Point A on Addendum B. This is where a person would begin the restorative process. Discuss the three aspects of Personal Discovery and why each one is important.

   Coming out of denial:


   Identifying problems:


   Exerting control over addictions:


2. What are some instances or situations in life that might need to be grieved?




3. Discuss some of the benefits of grieving your pain.




4. The keys to rebuilding are listed on Point B in Addendum B. Briefly discuss the importance of each one.

Recap...—#4

Understanding personal identity:

Working on developmental tasks:

Learning relational skills:

Trying new ways of thinking:

Giving self and others more grace:

Creating a healthy support system:

## LOOKING AT REAL LIFE:

5. Each individual will go through the restorative process differently. The length of time it takes to get from Point A to Point B varies from person to person. Can you think of an example of this in another person's life or in your own life?

Guided Discussion

## LOOKING AT MY LIFE:

As you've answered and discussing questions from *How Emotional Problems Develop* in this session and the previous three sessions, what is one thing you have learned?

How have you started to apply it to your own life?

# For Further Discussion
# Case Study #3

*Peter's wife Sarah asked him if they could go to marriage counseling because she hardly saw him anymore and wanted to leave him. Because he did not want to lose her, he reluctantly agreed to go.*

*Their counselor, Dr. Morris, asked Peter some questions about his childhood. After he heard Peter's story, Dr. Morris wanted to meet for six weeks with Peter to help him work on his individual issues. Peter told Dr. Morris that he came from a very loving and successful family and that he had problems but that his parents did not have any. Dr. Morris asked him why he works so much and Peter said that he wants to provide for his family. He asked Peter if he had any friends whom he had told about his depression. Peter replied, "No one wants to hear about that. Everyone wants me to be successful."*

*Dr. Morris encouraged Peter to join a Restoring Your Heart (RYH) group. When Peter first joined the group he was very nervous and did not want to share much. As time went by and he heard several of the other members of the group open up about their problems, he began to talk more. He began to realize that he was mad at his father. As he began to feel this anger and sadness about his childhood, he actually felt more depressed and angry at first. For a short period of time he was more apt to lose his temper with his wife or one of his employees. He began to grieve the fact that he had felt under tremendous pressure from his parents to do well in school and sports. He realized that he had never enjoyed sports as much as he should have been able to because of this pressure. He also realized he had spent too much time studying and had not had a chance to play as much as he should have. He was grieving the loss of parts of his childhood.*

*Dr. Morris helped him realize he had been working so much in the past as a way of avoiding his real feelings. Peter decided to cut back on work and spend more time with his family. He also began to control his anger better and appeared to be less driven. Instead of being happy about this, it actually made his employees nervous. They were afraid that the business might not do as well. Even his wife was nervous about the "new Peter" as he became more vulnerable and started to share his feelings more with her. But after she discussed this with Dr. Morris, she felt better about the situation and decided to have personal counseling herself.*

## CASE STUDY #3 — QUESTIONS FOR DISCUSSION

1) Did Peter appear to be getting better in all areas at first?

2) What insights did Peter gain about himself?

3) How did other people react to the changes in Peter?

# Next Steps For RYH
(After Participating in the 4-Week Study):

We hope you have gained new insights into your own life and the lives of those around you as you've completed the guided discussions for *How Emotional Problems Develop*. You may be wondering what to do with everything you've learned.

Many people choose to address the emotional issues they have recognized during this study by joining a Restoring Your Heart (RYH) group called *Processing Pain*, developed by the Restorative Ministry of Worldwide Discipleship Association. Others going through this material realize they have found their calling and want to use the information they've received to help others. In either case, the place to start is by going through a gender specific RYH group. To join a group, please contact us at restoringyourheart.com, or check with the leader of your group to find out if RYH groups are offered at your local church.

# Next Steps For Phase IV

For those who are interested in developing as a new leader, we suggest that you continue to work through the WDA materials listed in the "Introduction To Phase IV" at the beginning of this book. Resources can be found at www.disciplebuilding.org/store.

# Answers To The Guided Discussions

Leaders should read "Leader's Instructions For Using Guided Discussions," located at the beginning of this book, before facilitating a small group. Leaders also need to read the following notes and answers before the meeting where the specific lesson will be discussed. The suggested answers will guide the leader to what the main emphasis of the answer should be based on the topic of the Guided Discussion. Here they will also find suggestions, cautions and additional helpful information.

# 1 Understanding Root Causes Of Emotional Problems

3. *By processing it—feel it, learn from it. Paul says there is fruit from suffering. If we replace the word "pain" for "sufferings," the verse would read like this, "We also glory in our 'pain' because we know that 'pain' produces perseverance, perseverance character, and character hope." Pain, when handled correctly, can have a positive impact on our lives.*

4. *Give permission and provide a safe environment where the child can express emotions, use praise and positive language, give appropriate responsibilities for the child's age, treat the child with respect, stop any abusive behavior, give appropriate positive attention, give the child reasonable limits and boundaries, model dealing with pain in healthy ways, etc.*

5. *Society is impacted by drug and alcohol problems, broken families, teen pregnancies, etc., all of which are the result of emotional problems.*

6. *The church is impacted, just as the society is, by drug and alcohol problems, broken families, teen pregnancies, etc. These problems can lead to disagreements in churches, gossip, church*

*splits, etc.*

# 2 Healing From Emotional Issues

1. *Can affect relationships, decision-making, mental health, relationship with God, success in vocation, etc.*

2. *Bonding, Separating, Sorting Out Good and Bad, Gaining Independence*

   Bonding: *Problems connecting with others, problems trusting, unaware of feelings and needs, denies need for others*

   Separating: *Identity confusion, general lack of direction in life, boundary problems (too dependent on others, too isolated from others, overly responsible for others)*

   Sorting Out Good and Bad: *Blames self for everything bad that happens, denies their ability to contribute anything good, has difficulty acknowledging own faults, blames others, may initially see a situation/person as "all good," but after problems sees situation/person as "all bad."*

   Gaining Independence: *Continues to be dependent on parents or other adults, feels "one down" to other adults, has an inordinate need for approval, needs permission, has feelings of inferiority, gives away power to others, idealizes people in authority, fears failure*

3. Stop abusive relationships: *Just surviving in an abusive situation takes all of a person's energy. Therefore, in order to have the energy and motivation to grow and heal the person must be free from the abuse.*

   Control addictions: *If a person has severe addictions, they will not be able to work on emotional issues until these are under control. Severe addictions consume a person and prevent them from being able to deal with their emotions since addictions medicate emotions.*

Learn to view and express emotions properly: *Many people need to learn how to get in touch with their present emotions before they are able to deal with buried emotions.*

Grieve pain and losses: *Grieving losses will significantly reduce internal stress and the ill-effects of buried emotions.*

Understand needs and how to get them met appropriately: *Most people who have significant emotional issues have little awareness of what their real needs are or how to get them met. People must take responsibility for their own needs and for getting them met.*

Learn to distinguish between healthy and unhealthy thinking and behavior: *It is important to compare healthy and unhealthy family systems and relational patterns so we can recognize what is unhealthy and can make good choices rather than follow our programming from childhood.*

Develop a correct view of self, the world and God: *Underlying most unhealthy behavior is a distorted belief system, and it is important to correct the wrong and distorted views.*

Develop healthy relationships and a healthy support system: *Everyone needs a safe and caring support system where they can be totally honest about who they are and be totally accepted at the same time. Only when people can be fully honest and transparent can the wounds begin to heal.*

Learn to grow spiritually: *The more Christ is involved in the recovery process, the faster healing takes place.*

# 3 The Church's Role In Restoration

1. *Preach good news, bind up the broken hearted, proclaim freedom for the captives, release the prisoners, proclaim the year of the Lord's favor, comfort those who mourn, etc. To summarize, He wanted to bring healing to His people. He envisioned restoration being a major part of His ministry.*

2. *Christians should expect to become "oaks of righteousness." This is an image of strength and steadiness (vs. 3). They will rebuild the ancient ruins and restore places that are devastated. That is, they will be equipped to impact the healing and restoration of their community (vs. 4).*

3. *The church should be actively helping people heal from emotional problems.*

5. *No. It is helpful for the church to offer some resources such as a RYH group and/or a support group, but no one institution can be expected to do everything. The goal of the church should be to oversee the healing process and help the person find help, wherever it is.*

6. *Specific resources will vary from community to community. Sources to investigate are Christian counselors and psychiatrists, addiction groups (e.g. AA), RYH groups, books and magazine articles, counseling programs in churches, mental health clinics, telephone yellow pages, the internet, etc. Networking is important!!*

7. *Be a part of someone's support system, recognize symptoms in someone, get training to be a RYH group leader, be sensitive to hurting people, etc.*

# 4 Recap Of *How Emotional Problems Develop*

## GETTING STARTED:

*Learned more about the company and how it functioned (read Policy Manual, signed up for insurance, etc.)*
*Learned how the company wanted me to do the job*
*Developed new skills*
*Knew who my boss was and learned what the expectations were*
*Over time, earned boss's trust, likewise, my boss learned to trust my work and me*
*Learned how to fit in to a team and my role in it*
*Needed to actually work in the job in order to truly become competent. Experience is very important.*

1. Coming out of denial: *If we don't admit and name the problem, we will not deal with it, and it will continue to get worse and worse.*

   Identifying problems: *Identifying our problem helps us take responsibility for it and provides the motivation to deal with it.*

   Exerting control over addictions: *If addictions are not dealt with, they will hinder or undo any progress made in another area.*

2. *Need to grieve anything that involves experiencing loss. Examples include loss of financial stability; loss of employment; loss of a friend, a child, a spouse, a co-worker, etc.; loss of physical health and/or ability; loss of the ability to communicate; loss of childhood; loss of opportunities; loss of hope; loss of independence, etc.*

3. *Stress is relieved because emotions are released*
   *Enables you to reach forgiveness*
   *You learn how to express and release negative emotions in healthy ways*

*You feel better physically*
*Enables you to give up unhealthy defense mechanisms and addictions*
*Gives you the ability to see people and their problems more realistically*
*You learn how to show empathy*
*You have more energy*

4. **Understanding personal identity:** *Helps us know who we are; gives purpose and significance; helps us feel good about self; helps us have realistic expectations and allows us to make wise decisions*

    **Working on developmental tasks:** *Gives us skills to establish healthy relationships and develop right thinking*

    **Learning relational skills:** *This leads to healthier and deeper relationships*

    **Trying new ways of thinking:** *Allows a person to experience transformation*

    **Giving self and others more grace:** *Allows us to be human (flawed) and see others as human; allows us to be who we are without fear of rejection; allows us to be transparent*

    **Creating a healthy support system:** *Everyone needs support; no one does well when isolated*

# About WDA

WDA's mission is to serve the church worldwide by developing Christlike character in people and equipping them to disciple others according to the pattern Jesus used to train His disciples.

Organized as Worldwide Discipleship Association (WDA) in 1974, we are based in the United States and have ministries and partners throughout the world. WDA is a 501c(3) non-profit organization funded primarily by the tax-deductible gifts of those who share our commitment to biblical disciple building.

WDA is committed to intentional, progressive discipleship. We offer a flexible, transferable approach that is based on the ministry and methods of Jesus, the Master Disciple Builder. By studying Jesus' ministry, WDA discovered five phases of Christian growth. The Cornerstone series focuses on the first and second phases, Phase I: Establishing Faith and Phase II: Laying Foundations. Cornerstone addresses the needs of a young Christian or a more mature Christian who wants a review of foundational Christian truths. The Equipping For Ministry phase (Phase III) is geared toward disciples who are ready to learn how to minister to others. Phase IV: Developing New Leaders equips a person to take responsibility for the spiritual development and well-being of others while Phase V: Developing Mature Leaders expands the training of mature leaders.

For more information about WDA and disciple building, please visit our website: www.disciplebuilding.org.

The following materials are available at the WDA store.
www.disciplebuilding.org/store

### Maturity Matters®
Read *Maturity Matters®* by Bob Dukes.

Leaders must understand, balance, and apply the dynamics that contribute to progressive growth and sanctification. This requires both a strong faith and a new focus. As we fix our eyes on things unseen, the outcome will be a deeper faith, drawn in part from church leaders who consistently equip Christians. As we help them put truth into practice, faith grows. The rewards are both temporal and eternal.

### Disciple Building: A Biblical Framework
Read *A Biblical Framework* by Bob Dukes.

This book presents the philosophical overview of the discipleship ministry of Christ and how its principles can be applied to disciple building today.

### Cornerstone
Begin to build disciples using Cornerstone.

WDA Cornerstone features 38 Bible lessons and essays that help new Christians grow to maturity. These lessons cover the first two phases of growth, Establishing Faith and Laying Foundations. The Cornerstone curriculum is designed to run for approximately one year. Once established, it runs continuously with various entry points. Ideally, it works in concert with Life Coaches, who meet with and help orient disciples to the Christian life and the church community, facilitating and supplementing their involvement in a Discipleship Community.

**Phase III: Equipping For Ministry**
Equip disciples to minister to others.

WDA's Equipping For Ministry consists of 7 workbooks and manuals that feature content focusing on character and skills. The topics in this phase can be approached individually or in sequence. Disciples will learn about healthy relationships, spiritual warfare, positional truth, ministry principles, evangelism and inductive Bible study.

At the Equipping For Ministry Phase (III) a disciple has a strong personal relationship with God and has matured to the point that he is ready to begin having a ministry in the life of another person. Training at this phase is best done in a team of disciples who learn and do ministry together with an experienced discipleship leader.

**Life Coaching**
Learn how to be a Life Coach.

Life Coaches are Christian leaders who are willing to invest their knowledge and experience and even their very lives so that others might learn to think, feel and act like Jesus. A spiritual Life Coach is a person who, in the midst of a caring relationship, imparts truth that changes the life (conduct/character) of another, gradually helping the disciple become more like Jesus Christ. At WDA, we often use the phrase, "meeting people where they are, helping them take the next step®" to describe the Life Coaching process. Life Coach training offers a philosophical and practical approach that is carried out through the design and implementation of growth projects tailored to individual needs and levels of maturity.

WDA is able to provide Life Coach training in three distinct ways: individual self-study using our *Disciple Building: Life Coaching* manual, group study and interaction at a Life Coaching Seminar or through a 28/20® church ministry consulting relationship. To learn more about Life Coaching go to www.disciplebuilding.org/ministries/church-ministry/life-coaching

Watch the Life Coaching Introductory Video: https://vimeo.com/135056845

### Restoring Your Heart

Read *How Emotional Problems Develop.*

Through our experiences discipling people over the years, we at WDA have discovered that unresolved relational and emotional issues from the past can be a stumbling block to spiritual growth.

Our Restorative Ministry trains people in churches and in other ministries to help people through a healing process that will enable them to become healthier in all their relationships, including their relationship with God.

Check out **Restoring Your Heart** at www.restoringyourheart.com.

# WDA Partnership

## Help us build disciples worldwide.

**You can help us fulfill the great commission by becoming a Worldwide Discipleship Association (WDA) partner.** WDA's mission is to serve the church worldwide by developing Christlike character in people and equipping them to disciple others according to the pattern Jesus used to train His disciples.

Since our inception in 1974 our materials and processes have been used in more than 90 U.S. cities and in over 55 countries. We have created over a million direct discipleship impacts and have conducted face-to-face training to over 17,000 pastors and leaders around the globe! **Your support of WDA is vital to the success of our mission.** We pledge to serve as faithful stewards of your generous gifts to the ministry.

**www.disciplebuilding.org/give/wda-partnership**

## Become a Partner Today

**WDA**
WORLDWIDE DISCIPLESHIP ASSOCIATION

Made in the USA
Columbia, SC
12 February 2025